Etsy SEO

REVEALED

A no-nonsense guide to help you take your Etsy SEO & business to the next level

TABLE OF CONTENTS:

THE BEGINNING…

I started my Etsy journey 7 years ago. It seemed like an easy to use platform and I wanted to try it out. At the time I had just started my small clothing company and was only selling on eBay. I'm the type of person that jumps right in and doesn't overthink things too much. I put up 20 listings and gave no real thought to my titles or tags. I think my titles had 4 or 5 words in them. My tags had about the same, if any. Skip forward a few months and no sales later I was like what the heck. I did the work by spending time listing these products, now buy them and give me money. They're good! Buy them dammit!

Well, as I quickly realized if no one was seeing my listings how were they going to buy. Throwing up listings with a few generic, basic keywords wasn't going to cut it. I needed to rethink what I was doing and stop half-assing my listings. I needed to put my full ass into it. I started to do a lot of SEO research to find out what the top shops were doing and what the best practices were. I tested and analyzed my shop and made changes when necessary. I was consistent and took a lot of action.

Fast forward a few months later I had a few dozen sales under my belt. I was super excited and knew that I could make money on Etsy. Customers existed that were going to buy MY STUFF. Very cool. I ended up finishing my first year on Etsy with about $4,000 in sales. It wasn't easy, but it was worth it. That extra money helped me pay bills and gave me extra spending money.

Now, 6 years later, as a top 1% Etsy seller I've learned a ton about Etsy. I've opened up several Etsy shops for myself and other clients. I have also personally coached dozens of Etsy sellers to help them turn their Etsy shops into successful businesses. I've learned what works and what doesn't work, especially when it comes to SEO. I see many other new and veteran Etsy sellers struggle because they haven't found their way yet. I've seen people who sell amazing products leave or quit altogether. It's frustrating to me because I know they could sell their stuff if they implemented the strategies I've learned over the years. My goal is to change your path and help you find the success on Etsy I know you're capable of achieving.

WHAT IS SEO?

Let's start at the ground level. If you don't know what SEO is, what it does or what it means, don't worry. You will know all that very soon. No fluff, let's get to it.

SEO stands for search engine optimization. To simplify it even more, it's basically how customers find your shop and products. There are specific key factors that help more customers find you. This is the ultimate goal for all of us! Don't zone out on me yet. SEO isn't hard. What makes it challenging is that many people don't take the time to understand the fundamentals, their customers or niche. There are also a lot of variables to consider. My goal is to simplify SEO as much as possible for you and give you actionable strategies to immediately help your shop succeed.

WHAT IMPACTS ETSY SEO?

With any e-commerce site, different factors impact how customers find you. Luckily, you only have to worry about Etsy SEO.

First, your Etsy shop sections impact overall SEO. How? Think of it this way. Your shop sections add a professional and complete element to your store. Would you shop at Target if there wasn't a Target sign out front? No, you wouldn't know what store it was. Your Etsy shop is no different. It's important to fill out ALL of your shop sections so it looks professional. More than that Etsy likes to send buyers to complete shops. So having your shop sections filled out is twofold. What do I mean by shop sections? This includes your logo, banner image, announcement section, shop members, about, and shop policies. I'll dive into some tips to help you with your shop sections in the next segment.

Next, your listing titles and keywords significantly impact SEO more than anything else. Why? Keywords are the words or phrases customers are using to find the products they want to buy. If you sell a product they want but do not have the keywords they're using when they search, they will never find your stuff. That's why it's soooo important to use the correct keywords and high-quality keywords to jump in front of those customers. I will hit on title and tag keywords heavily in a later section.

Also, categories and the category options you select impact SEO. This is because a seller has the option to filter what they want to buy and not use the search bar at all. If you don't have the right category for your product selected and are not using the category options, then you will not be found. Don't worry, I'll touch on this more in depth later as well.

Last, customer reviews impact SEO. Bad reviews can kill a shop's success in more ways than one. Enough bad reviews in a short period can cause your shop to be shut down by Etsy. Make sure you do everything possible to never get bad reviews, especially early on when you have little or no reviews to start with. Bad reviews are inevitable, but there are strategies you can use to help you minimize them. More to come on this in a later section.

Those are the main, known areas that impact Etsy SEO and your products being found on Etsy.

Note: Listing descriptions DO NOT impact SEO. At least not yet. However, don't slack on them. They are still very important for sales.

SHOP SECTIONS & SEO:

Like I said above, your Etsy shop sections impact SEO and how a customer perceives your shop. Your shop sections give customers their first impression. Do you want to give them a flea market impression or a Target impression? Not that flea markets are bad, I love them. But, if you've ever been to one crap is thrown everywhere with no focus on a quality presentation. This is why you can get great deals. Sellers don't care. Let's make a good first impression and have everything filled out with attention to detail. Below I'm going to touch on the important sections with some pointers.

Shop Logo: Your shop logo doesn't have to be complicated but it does need to be there. You can easily create your logo for free in canva.com or pay someone to do it for $5 on fiverr.com. It can be as easy as two letters that represent your shop name with a small graphic. Don't overthink it. If your shop name is Emily's Bows, do a small bow graphic with an EB. See simple. You're killin' it already!

Banner Image: This can be a bigger logo or just be a collection of your products. A well put together banner image looks great for an Etsy shop. A missing one is no bueno. You can use the same resources I mentioned above to create this.

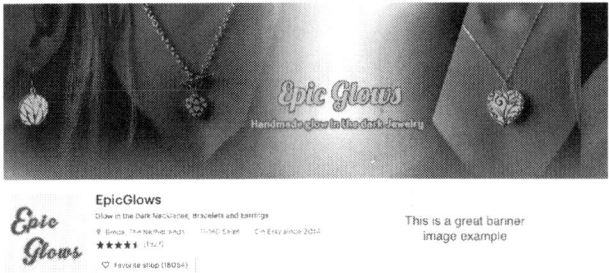

This is a great banner image example

Announcement section: This should be a short sentence welcoming buyers to your

This is the type of stuff that should go in your announcement section

shop or some pertinent information such as shipping deadlines. Don't put a book about your shop in this section. That's where your about section comes in. See below for that.

About section: This is where you put a paragraph or two talking about your shop, what you make and how you got started. It should be professional, personable and real. Please for the love of God don't complain or be negative in this section. It's not a good look. Etsy buyers like to learn more about who they're buying from.

Shop members: This should be super simple but needs to be done. If it's just you working on your shop just add yourself with an owner title. If you have others helping add them with their titles. Feel free to make this section your own and be creative. A little humor helps too.

Shop members

The PJP Team
Owner

I originally started Puddle Jumper Pups after unsuccessfully trying to find the perfect combo of stylish, yet durable collars for my own dogs, Millie, Hattie and Otto. We hope you enjoy the shop!

Sunny
Lead Seamstress

Sunny is our lead seamstress on the PJP Team. When Sunny is not working hard you can find her playing outdoors with her teacup yorkie Emily and Australian Shepard Bonnie. Sunny has been part of the PJP team since 2014.

Monica
Assistant, Customer Service

Monica is part of our Customer Service team. While Monica does not own a pup herself she does love to spoil her little french bulldog niece. Monica has been part of the PJP team since 2014.

Here is an example of an excellent shop member section

Shop Policies: This is a MUST. Please make sure to fill this out. Etsy makes it super easy by already having default policies in this section that you just have to activate. Customers always want to know processing times and refund policies. Don't short change them on this. You can easily use or edit the default policies already there and save yourself a lot of time. It takes less than a minute. I can assure you no one will buy your stuff if they do not know if they can return it.

Shop policies
Last updated on

Accepted payment methods

Accepts Etsy Gift Cards and Etsy Credits

Never leave your policies blank

KEYWORDS:

Alright, this is the meat and potatoes of this guide. This is where Etsy heroes are made. I mean I think you're already a hero, but now you can be an Etsy sales hero too. Let's break down keywords and get you some good info to take your shop to the next level.

WHAT ARE KEYWORDS?

Keywords are the words/phrases used in your listing title and tags to help customers find products which they are searching for. Keywords are the lifeblood of your listing and the most important. Please keep in mind that you can use the best keywords in the world, but if your product or listing is junk you still won't get sales. Make sure you have good pictures and are selling quality products at the right price. I know that was blunt, but you want sales right?

LONG TAIL KEYWORDS:

This term will be relevant to what comes next, so I want to explain it now. A long tail keyword per Etsy is 3 or more words or phrases put together to form a keyword. So don't get confused, it's not just one word. For example, necklace is not a long tail keyword. Blue opal pendant gold necklace is a long tail keyword. You want to try and use as many relevant long tail keywords as possible because they're usually more specific to your product. Necklace is a very broad term and there will be millions of listings for that keyword when you search. If you get more specific to what you're selling by using long tail keywords, there is a better chance of the customers searching for what you're selling finding you. Thus, this gives you more traffic and creates a better buying experience. I'll touch on this more in the following sections, but that should give you a good overview of long tail keywords.

One word keyword vs. long tail keyword search result examples:

Necklace = 4,853,756 search results

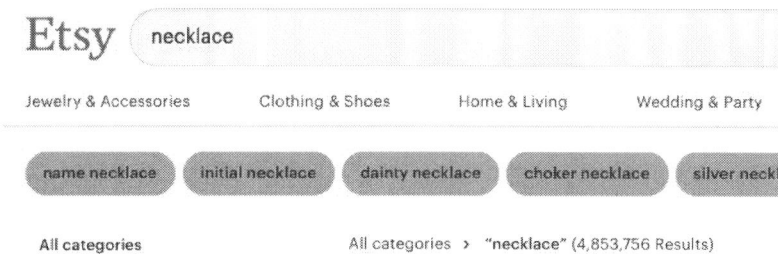

Blue opal pendant gold necklace = 3,361 search results

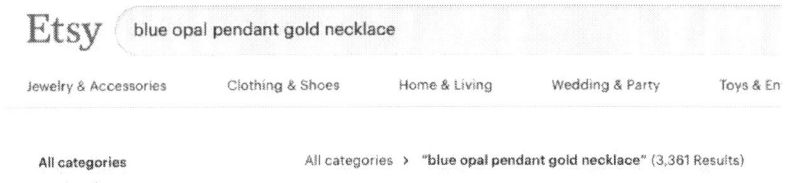

Etsy   blue opal pendant gold necklace

Jewelry & Accessories   Clothing & Shoes   Home & Living   Wedding & Party   Toys & En

All categories

All categories > "blue opal pendant gold necklace" (3,361 Results)

TITLE KEYWORDS:

Your title has a 160 character limit for keywords including spaces. Your goal should be to fill up most of the title with high-quality keywords related to what you're selling. A good way to set up your title is to use the strongest, highest quality long tail keyword first. Also, keep in mind that your first keyword long tail or not gets the most weight with Etsy search. Meaning keywords that occur in the front of your title are ranked higher. So don't put good keywords last. Get Baby out of the corner and put her first! You can also separate keywords by commas, dashes, or slashes. Some people choose not to do this. I haven't found much of a difference in performance, however, there are some benefits to what you choose. Commas make it easier to copy keywords to your tags because it will automatically separate them when you press enter. Dashes look prettier but take up more space if you use spaces between each dash. I usually use commas or dashes because I don't want my title to look like a big run-on sentence of nonsense or at least less of one. So, it's up to you and mostly a personal preference. Now you're ready to complete your title. You know your first keyword should be long tail . Keep in mind it can be more than 3 words. For example: gold chain blue opal pendant necklace. This would be an awesome long tail keyword. Anyone that searched for that exact term would probably find your listing. Also, those that searched gold chain or opal pendant necklace or gold pendant necklace or gold chain opal would all have a chance of finding you even though they are broader keywords. They are still part of your long tail keyword and will still pull up in Etsy search. Now that you have the first long tail keyword done, you will next need to continue to fill out your title with additional high-quality keywords long tail or not. Use up all your long tail keywords first, then if you run out move on to whatever additional keywords you have left.

Example: Gold Chain Blue Opal Pendant Necklace, gold chain opal accessory, small opal pendant, natural opal necklace, opal gift

The goal is to try and use different terms that still relate to your item. You wouldn't put anything unrelated or too broad in your title. For example, I wouldn't put jewelry. That's way too broad. However, I could put opal necklace jewelry and that would be a decent long tail keyword.

TAG KEYWORDS:

Now it's time to move onto your tags. You should use the same strategy as you did for your title. However, there are some slight differences. First, the order of your tags doesn't matter. Etsy does not give more SEO weight to tags that are first as opposed to last. Next, you have to work within the confines of a 22 character tag limit per tag. This includes spaces. For this reason, some of your keywords may not fit. A good strategy for tags is to copy the same keywords you used in your title down to your tags. You will run into the problem of them not all fitting because of that character limit like I just mentioned. If this happens you can split the tags up. For Example: Gold Chain Blue Opal Pendant Necklace will not fit. You can split this up into two or three tags.

Example: Gold Chain Blue Opal, Opal Pendant, Pendant Necklace, etc.

These are just some of the ways you could arrange the tags. Try not to go too broad if you can help it.

Example: Gold Chain, Opal, Pendant, Necklace

These terms by themselves are very broad. You can help make them better quality by combining related terms together for a higher quality tag. Chances are you will have additional tags remaining after you add all of the keywords from your title because there are 13 spots. Try to think of completely different keywords you can use. If you really can't think of any additional keywords use different combinations of existing keywords. Honestly, the Etsy search algorithm is supposed to analyze all of your keywords together and cross-reference them with customer searches to present the most related product to what that customer is looking for. If this is the case, ultimately the combinations of tags may not matter if they are all related to your product. I still like to lay them out in a way that makes sense to how people would search for my item. This has worked well for me thus far.

KEYWORD RESEARCH:

You now know the best practices for setting up your title and tags. You go to implement these amazing strategies and instantly run out of keyword ideas. Crap! No worries, I'm here to save your day. Let's talk about some ways to brainstorm and find new keywords to use.

The first place I want you to start is within Etsy. There are a few ways to get help this way. The first is to start with yourself. No, I haven't lost my mind. Sometimes the best keywords are in our listing descriptions. When we write our descriptions we often come up with excellent ways of describing our products because we're thinking about our customers and making sure they have all the details. Well, as a side effect this also gives us some pretty darn good keywords. I've seen this many times with shop owners. So if you have a description done, go back and look through it for more keywords to use. You'd be surprised.

If you can't help yourself then proceed to the Etsy search bar. This is a great resource to find additional keywords. If you start typing in a word it will automatically start populating keywords related to your search. These are usually highly searched keywords. Keep trying different combinations to see what comes up.

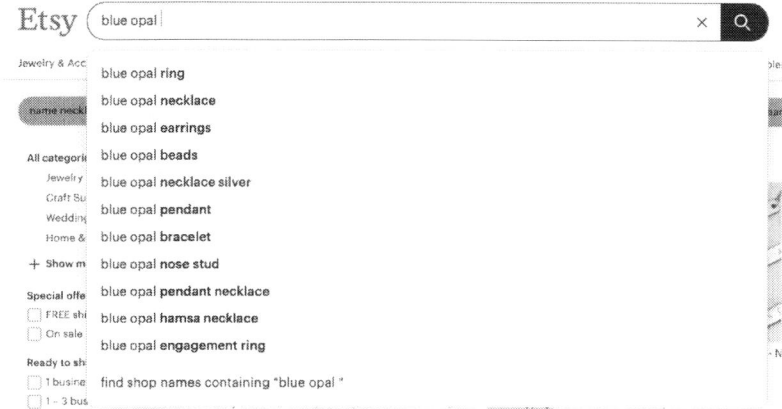

The next thing you can do is look at related listings. While we don't want to steal our competitor's ideas, NOT COOL, we can use their keywords to give us ideas that we can apply to our products.

You can also use google to help give you ideas. You can do the search bar trick with google. This may be a little more challenging depending on your niche. You can also use the google keyword planner. I believe you have to sign up for a google ads account now to get the planner. It's free. You only pay money if you run ads. The google ads planner allows you to see search traffic for whatever keywords you enter into it. It will also give you related keywords. I wouldn't go all-in on this one because the traffic is different from Etsy, but the big search terms should still work for you.

The last thing you can do is get third-party help from Etsy SEO platforms. There are two main ones. www.erank.com and marmalead.com. Both are pretty good. I've used both, but prefer Erank a little more. They are great for giving you keyword ideas and letting you see search traffic, engagement, and competition. If you do use these please do not let this be your end all be all to keywords. Many people get in the weeds and only use the search terms they find on these platforms. They forget to think like the customer and become robotic. They also get distracted and spend too much time on keywords. It should only take you a few minutes per listing on your title and tags. If you're spending hours researching keywords you're doing it wrong. Also, the more you get to know your customers and niche, the better at coming up with great keywords you'll become.

ADVANCED SEO STRATEGIES:

You've read all the best practices above and you're thirsty for more! I got you. Let's talk about some advanced strategies that you can implement down the road to help your shop's performance. Keep in mind everything I talk about I've done and it has worked well for me. I am not blowing smoke and wouldn't want you to waste your time. I would also suggest that you do not try this stuff right out of the gate. Get your business going first and make sure you have a good handle on the basics. There is no need to run a 5k when you haven't run a mile yet. Let's not puke everywhere quite yet. Or in other words, let's not get overwhelmed. The first strategy is testing testing testing. With marketing, it's important to test. Etsy is no different. You can test anything and monitor performance. I am going to keep this test related to Etsy SEO. Here is how you test using keywords. First, duplicate your listing. You will now have two identical listings. Next, you will change either the title or the keywords of the duplicated listing. I would not suggest changing both because if you do you won't know what worked or didn't work because you changed two things. Let's say you decide to change your title. Erase all of your keywords. Now you can either use completely different keywords relating to your product or you can rearrange your existing keywords or you can use a combination of new and rearranged keywords. Whatever you choose, still use the strategies I talked about in the listing SEO section to set up your title. Now publish. From there you can monitor that listing's performance in the stats section compared to your first listing. Keep it active for 1-4 months. Keep an eye on visits to see if it's getting more or less traffic. And of course, keep an eye on sales and ultimately conversion.

Important Definitions:

Visits = The number of unique individuals looking at your listing or shop (focus on these over views)

Views = The number of times an individual looks at your listings. An individual can look at different items or the same item more than once inflating this number. (Focus on visits over views because visits are more relevant because we want as many unique visitors as possible)

Conversion = The number of sales divided by the number of visits (a conversion above 1% is good)

If your tested listing performs badly you can choose to deactivate it. If it does well you can choose to keep it active and delete your original listing. Or on the off chance both do well you can keep them both active. I would suggest leaving it up for at least a month to see how it performs. Honestly, you've already paid .20 cents to list it so you might as well keep it up for the renewal cycle then decide what you want to do. You can do the same test with listing tags. The key is not to keep changing your listings before they have time to run through the algorithm. Have faith and let them ride for a while (at least a month) until you make another change.

Another SEO strategy you can use is to capitalize on seasonal or holiday keywords. Think about what you're selling and if any of your products could have a seasonal element. From there you can either change the existing listing's title/tags or create new listings using your different seasonal keywords. For example, if you sell custom wallets and father's day is coming up you can capitalize on these keywords to market your product. Here are some specific examples: Father's Day Leather Wallet, father's day wallet gift, wallet gift for dad, handmade wallet for dad, etc.

You can also use Etsy stats to help you capitalize on good keywords that are performing well for you. Go into the stats tab, then scroll down to your listings and click on one. You will see specific stats for that listing such as views, visits, revenue, etc. Scroll down until you see search terms. It will rank all of your search terms from most visits to least visits. While you don't know how many buyers you have from each search term, you can see how many people are finding your product from that specific term. It's safe to assume that terms with a high number of visits are pretty good to use. I would then see if you have terms with high visits that you can apply to other listings. This way you can spread the wealth. You may have an awesome search term that could apply to 5 listings, but you're only using it for one. I would focus on the terms with over 50 visits or more.

(Example of how individual listing keyword stats look. The higher the total visits the better the keyword)

Search terms
ⓘ Updated Just now

What search terms are people using to find your shop or listings? Use these as ideas for listing tags.

SEARCH TERMS	ETSY	GOOGLE, ETC.	TOTAL VISITS
yoga gifts	36	57	93
yoga shirt	26	12	38
yoga	-	35	35
funny yoga shirt	12	3	15

LISTING CATEGORIES & CATEGORY OPTIONS:

Another largely forgotten aspect of SEO is listing categories. This is how you categorize your product such as wall art, clothing, decals, etc. You can type whatever your product is in the category search bar of your listing and select from the available categories that pop up. Some products may fit in multiple categories. You have to decide which category is best for your product or list items in multiple categories. Right under the categories section, you'll find a variety of additional dropdown options to select from that help describe your product. The category options are different for each category. The only dropdown options that remain the same are "occasion" and "holiday". No matter what dropdown options show up for

These are optional category options you can choose.
Always fill these out if they apply.

your category, it is very important that you select all applicable options relating to what you're selling. Here's why. Some people do not type search terms in the Etsy search bar, but rather search by categories on the main page of Etsy. It is possible to add filters and find exactly what you're looking for by filtering down your selections. If you do not have your category options filled out you may get filtered out. This will cause a group of customers to never even have the option to see your products. SEO is a lot about increasing your chances of being seen. What keywords you use, what categories and category options you choose all can increase or decrease those chances. Let's increase your chances, shall we?

SHIPPING & SEO:

As some of you may already know Etsy recently made some changes regarding shipping as it relates to SEO. Simply put, if you choose to offer a free shipping guarantee for customer purchases over $35 your listings will get priority in Etsy search. It's like getting picked first for kickball. What this means is that if you and a competitor rank for the same keyword, your listing will be shown first if that competitor does not have the free shipping guarantee. I know some people have been upset about this so don't kill the messenger. My goal is to give you some tips on how to help leverage these changes to benefit you.

Why did Etsy make these changes? They surveyed a bunch of customers last year and found that most people said they were more prone to buy items that had free shipping. To stay competitive with other platforms they decided to push sellers towards free shipping by giving them priority in Etsy search.

Honestly, sellers should be offering some type of shipping incentive anyway. Even if you decided not to offer free shipping over $35, you should offer it for some amount. It entices customers to want to spend more. I don't know about you, but if I have to spend $10 more to save $5 or $10 in shipping, I'll try and find something else to buy. This marketing strategy has been around for a long time because it works.

Here are some things you can do to help with shipping costs. You can work some of all of the cost into your product cost. If you sell and item for $40 and your shipping is $5, you can then sell it for $45 and offer a free shipping guarantee. I've had some sellers say this is deceiving. Shipping is part of your production cost. If you choose to work that into your item cost and have free shipping or charge more for shipping and less for your item, that's up to you. Many customers think shipping costs can be deceiving because when they're ready to buy they get to the checkout page only to see $10 added to their cost. This is just how the e-commerce business works, like it or not. Just do your best to make it work for you and your margins.

If you sell products under $35, I would suggest keeping a shipping cost. Maybe you can make it slightly lower, but I would keep it. I tested free shipping with no minimum purchase and free shipping for over $35 and found little or no difference in sales. The only difference was in the money I lost by eating those shipping costs. Also, by offering free shipping with no minimum purchase you loose the incentive for customers to buy more. Another thing you can do to help save you some money is to buy shipping materials in bulk. If you can get your material costs down you can recuperate some of those costs. The last strategy I would suggest is to offer shipping upgrades on all of your orders. You can add upgrades for processing times and shipping types. Many customers will pay a few extra dollars to get their items shipped out faster and received faster. Here is an example. If your normal processing time is 3-5 days you can offer 1 day processing for $2.95. So even if they get free shipping, but buy the upgrade, you'll still get money for shipping. Or you can offer and upgrade for processing and mail type. An example of this would be 1 day processing and priority mail shipping for $10.95. They automatically get free shipping but buy the upgrade and in return you still get paid for shipping. You add these upgrades on your listing shipping profiles. This is a great way to not only offer your customers extra services, but also a way to earn extra revenue per order.

Shipping is always going to be a contentious topic, but these strategies should hopefully help you alleviate some of the pitfalls.

CUSTOMER REVIEWS:

You're going on vacation and looking for the perfect hotel. What's the first thing you do? Look up hotel reviews, right? At least most of us probably do this unless you're super adventurous and want to play hotel roulette. I'll take my chances with new coffee flavors, but not hotels. Reviews are everywhere and most people look at them before they decide to purchase. Etsy is no different. In addition to good reviews prompting a customer to buy from you, they also help with Etsy SEO. Etsy does not want to send customers to a shop with subpar reviews. No one is sure how much SEO weight is put behind your reviews, but we do know there is some. Below are some review tips to help you get more gold stars than you did elementary school.

Very Few Or No Reviews: Reviews are ALWAYS important, but they are extremely important when you are starting and have little or no reviews. The first reason they are important is because if you get a few bad reviews early on Etsy can suspend your shop. They have a threshold with shops based on how many bad reviews you have compared to good reviews. If that threshold gets too high in a certain period they'll shut your shop down. This applies to established shops as well but is important with newer shops because it's easier to meet that threshold. The current threshold is 1%, but as with anything that can change. Also, if your shop has 4 reviews and 2 are bad, customers will not want to buy from you. It will kill the potential to get new customers until your reviews get better which is hard since you're reviews are bad. It's a bad cycle to get into. It's way easier to not let it happen in the first place.

How To Avoid Bad Reviews: This may sound obvious, but I'm going to say it anyway. Make you are delivering a great product and a product as described. The easiest way people mess this up is by adding filters to their pictures which can change the color of your product.

Just make sure everything is the same color, same size, and the same quality you're describing.

Make sure you ship out products within your listed shipping times. Shipping items late is probably the most common way people get bad reviews. It's always better to ship items quicker than your listed shipping times. For example, if you select to ship items in 3-5 days, try to ship them out by day 3 or 4. If something happens where you have to ship out an item late, just message the buyer and let them know. Most of the time they're fine with it and appreciate the heads up. I've done this several times and never had an issue.

Offer great customer service. If someone reaches out before or after they buy to make sure you respond fast, are courteous and always thank them. If they're reaching out about an issue or problem after they buy to make sure you're doing everything possible to fix the issue or accommodate them. This is just good business.

What To Do If You Get A Bad Review: It's going to happen. If you're good, it may not happen for a while. It took me about 3 years to get my first bad review. I pride myself on keeping 5 stars and getting a bad review upset me. You have to try your best to take the emotion out of it, not take it personally, and move to solution mode. A bad review is not the end of the world. It can be fixed. Yay! Here's how. First, make sure you have the Sell on Etsy app installed on your phone. Second, make sure you have push notifications set up for reviews. You can set them up for sales, favorites and other stuff too. That can be distracting. The most important notification to set up for reviews so it prompts you to look at the review right away. It will show you good reviews which is cool. Pat yourself on the back or high five a stranger when you get those. What you need the notification for is on the off chance you get a bad review. If you do, you'll get the push notification and know right away. Once this happens stop what you're doing and respond to that customer right away. Apologize sincerely and offer a solution. It's best to offer a solution that's above and beyond what they're expecting. You are regaining their trust by wowing them first by responding to their review so fast and second by offering a "wow" solution. This is important for when you ask them to update their review which I'll get to soon. Here is an example of a normal solution. If they give you a bad review because their item arrived late you can offer to refund their shipping. An above and beyond solution would be to refund their shipping and also give them a refund on a percentage of their purchase. If the bad review isn't clear what the customer was upset about or you're not sure of the best solution, ask them what you can do to make it right. Most of the time coming up with a solution that will make them happy is doable. You may lose some money, especially if it was your fault, but it's worth it to make the customer happy. Now here is the key. Once you fix the problem reach back out to them and confirm they're satisfied. If so ask them if they'd mind updating their review and that you'd appreciate it if they did so. I haven't had many bad reviews, but following this process, I've gotten every bad review updated by the now satisfied customer. This could be a game-changer, especially if your shop is new. Customers appreciate when a company goes above and beyond to make things right. They are usually very understanding that mistakes happen. Take accountability, apologize, and make it right. it's as easy as that.

How To Get More Reviews: As you should know by now, reviews are really important. Now how do you get more reviews, especially when starting? Great question! I have a solution for that as well, but just because you're awesome.

I have found that only about 10% of customers leave a review. Most people just don't have the time or take the time to do so. This stinks when you are delivering great products because it takes a while to get a lot of reviews when only about 10% of customers are leaving them. Here is how you can work on getting that percentage up. In your shipping settings, you have the option of editing your packing slips. Your packing slip is what you should include in every customer package that's sent out. Etsy automatically generates them when you print out your labels. You can edit the top of your packing slip to say whatever you want. This is a great opportunity to ask customers to please leave a review if they're happy with their purchase. Tell them it would mean a lot to you and your shop. Also, make sure to tell them that if for some reason they're not satisfied to please reach out to you before leaving a review so you can make it right for them. This can help you eliminate bad reviews before they happen. It can also get you some more reviews. Another way to get reviews is to message buyers after they receive their items and pretty much follow the same process. You can message them something like, "I hope you're super happy with your (whatever product). If you could take a quick sec and leave a review I'd appreciate it." This is a more direct approach, but it can be very effective at getting more reviews quickly.

THIS IS THE END BUT NOT THE END...

I covered quite a bit in this book. Hopefully, I didn't make your head explode. Now comes the most important part of your journey. And that is... drum roll... to take action! Simple enough right? However, sadly, many people will not implement what they've learned and their shop will not improve or even worse, not even get off the ground. Set small, weekly goals for yourself. These should be specific and attainable. This will help you stay on track. One good goal would be to revamp some of your listings each week using the SEO strategies you've learned. So, now that you have a goal, make it specific. Example: I will update 5 of my listings with new SEO techniques each week. This is now a specific goal where you will easily know if you reached it or not at the end of the week. Do not get overwhelmed by trying to do everything at once. Focus on one goal, stick with that until it's complete and then set another goal. Maybe it takes you a month to update all your listings. Stick with that goal until all of your listings are updated, then set another goal for yourself. Where people fail is they try to do 10 things at once and never finish any of them.

"There is no failure except in no longer trying." - Chris Bradford

Good luck with your Etsy business going forward. I know that if you stay on the right path you will find success. Stay tuned for additional resources and dynamic ebooks that will continue to help you get to the next level.

Printed in Great Britain
by Amazon

55843661R00017